The Accident

MIKE WILSON

A car pulls up.
The man gets out,
and stands looking at the house.

No lights.
Where is she, he thinks,
has she walked out on me?

He walks up to the house,
slowly, with his head down.

She sits in the dark
and waits.
She doesn't move
when she hears the car.

All she can see
is the dim red glow
of her cigarette
burning like an angry, sleepless eye.

"Why have you started smoking again?"
It is the first thing he says to her.
She says nothing.

The house is cold.

"I thought you were out,"
he says,
"I thought you'd gone..."

He frowns in the dark.
Then he says softly:
"Sorry I'm late, love."

"Who is she?"
she says, cold and hard.

"What?"

"Who is she, Howard?
Is it someone I know?
Is it one of our friends?"

She says the word
as if it burns her lips.

Oh God, he thinks.
Here we go again.

"I have been in a traffic jam."
He speaks coldly, carefully.

"On the motorway.
A six-mile tail-back.
It took hours, Val..."

His legs are shaking.
He sits down.

"There was a car crash.
It was on the radio.
They said two people died.

"We all rolled slowly past
in our cars.
I saw the blood on the road.

"There was broken glass everywhere."
Like broken stars, he thought,
like broken dreams.

He sits with his head in his hands.

"I don't want you to live here any more," she says.

He looks up.

"I'm not seeing another woman, Val!"

But she isn't listening.

"I want you to move out now,"
she goes on,
"Tonight.
Get your things and go."

"I'm late home from work, Val," he shouts.
"It was an accident!"

She says:
"Marrying you, Howard.
That was the accident."

For five minutes,
no-one speaks.
There's not a sound in the house.

She is thinking:
ten years.
Ten years of my life.
What do you do
when the love's all gone?

And she thinks:
What about Danny?
Little Danny asleep upstairs.
What's going to happen to Danny?

Howard is thinking:
she's smoking again.
She knows I hate her smoking.
She's doing it just to get at me.

He says:
"You are, aren't you?
You're smoking that thing
just to get at me.
Just to make me angry!"

She flicks her cigarette at him.
It curves in the air
in the dark room
and hits him on the face.

He jumps back,
rubbing his cheek,
and the cigarette falls on the carpet.

It lies there, burning,
like an angry eye.

He doesn't move,
and he doesn't say anything.

He is thinking about Kim,
the new girl in the sales team,
and her warm, sexy smile.